HORSE — 30 MILES (48 KM) PER HOUR

SKATEBOARD — 15 MILES (24 KM) PER HOUR

DOG — 20 MILES (32 KM) PER HOUR

JET — 580 MILES (933 KM) PER HOUR   NOW THAT'S FAST!: JETS

JACKRABBIT — 45 MILES (72 KM) PER HOUR

HUMAN — 12 MILES (19 KM) PER HOUR

BICYCLE — 15 MILES (24 KM) PER HOUR

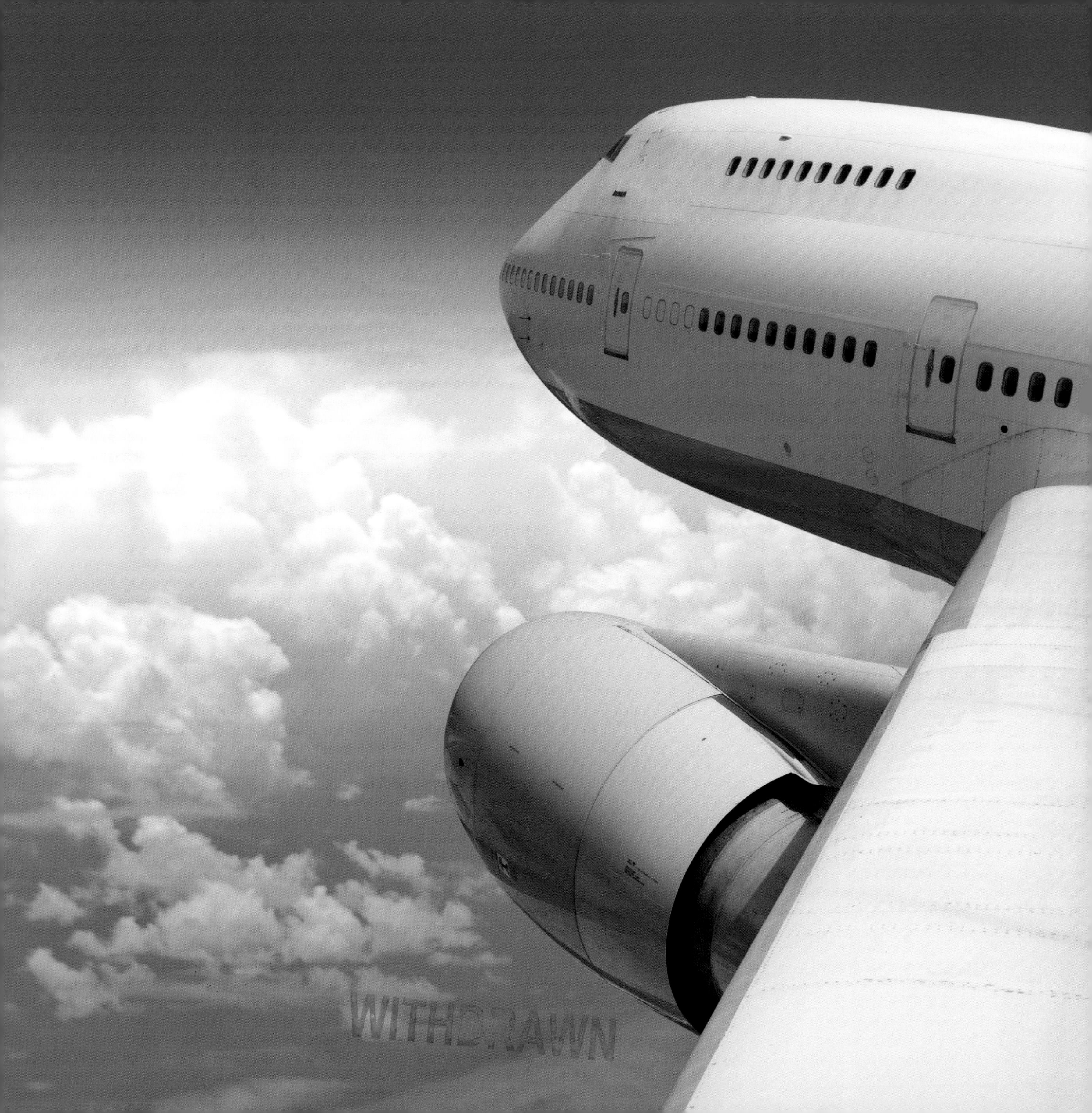

NOW THAT'S FAST!
JETS

KATE RIGGS

CREATIVE EDUCATION

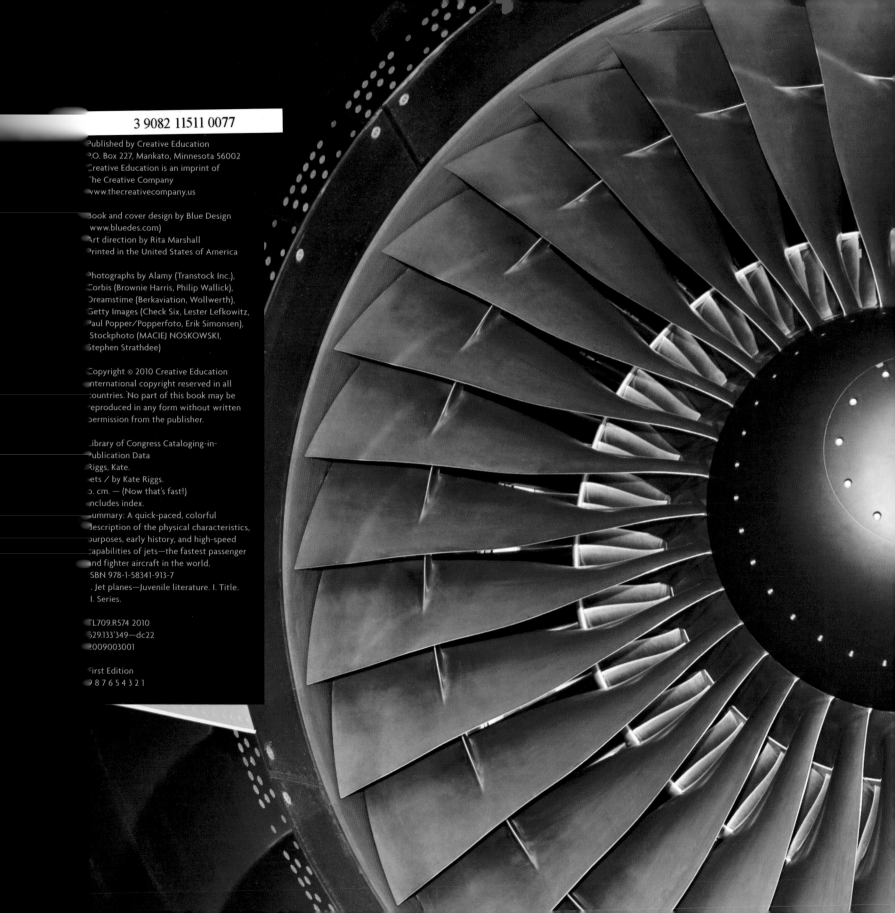

Published by Creative Education
P.O. Box 227, Mankato, Minnesota 56002
Creative Education is an imprint of
The Creative Company
www.thecreativecompany.us

Book and cover design by Blue Design
(www.bluedes.com)
Art direction by Rita Marshall
Printed in the United States of America

Photographs by Alamy (Transtock Inc.),
Corbis (Brownie Harris, Philip Wallick),
Dreamstime (Berkaviation, Wollwerth),
Getty Images (Check Six, Lester Lefkowitz,
Paul Popper/Popperfoto, Erik Simonsen),
Stockphoto (MACIEJ NOSKOWSKI,
Stephen Strathdee)

Library of Congress Cataloging-in-
Publication Data
Riggs, Kate.
Jets / by Kate Riggs.
p. cm. — (Now that's fast!)
Includes index.
Summary: A quick-paced, colorful
description of the physical characteristics,
purposes, early history, and high-speed
capabilities of jets—the fastest passenger
and fighter aircraft in the world.
ISBN 978-1-58341-913-7
1. Jet planes—Juvenile literature. I. Title.
II. Series.

TL709.R574 2010
629.133'349—dc22
2009003001

First Edition
9 8 7 6 5 4 3 2 1

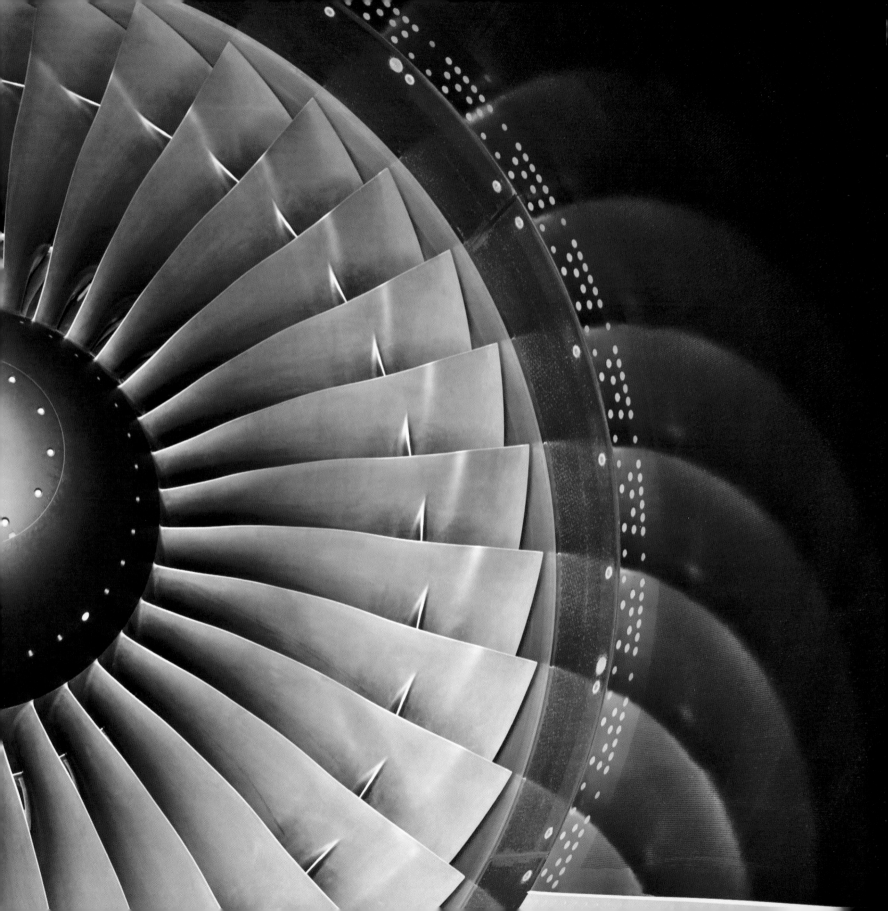

A jet is a high-powered airplane. Jets have strong **engines**. They can fly higher than other airplanes. They can fly faster, too. Most jets that carry a lot of people go about 580 miles (933 km) per hour. Other jets can go more than 1,300 miles (2,092 km) per hour!

Skilled people called engineers build and fix jet engines

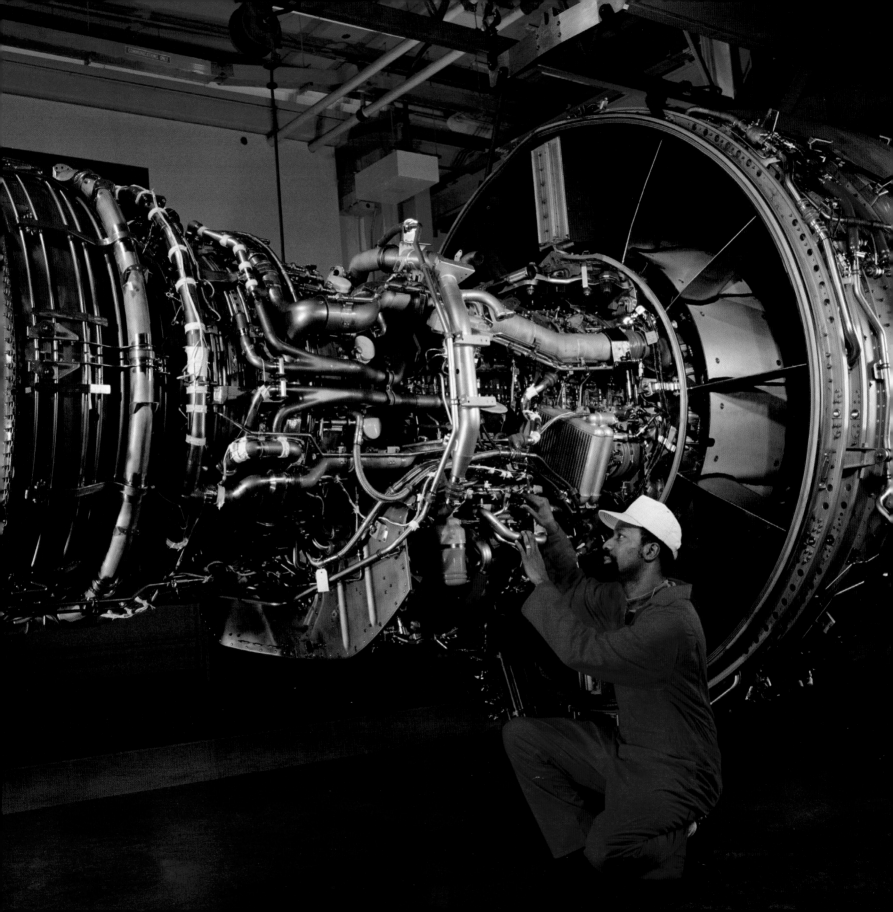

Most jets are used to fly **passengers** around the world. Some jets are small planes. They carry four or five people. Other jets can carry lots of people. These jets are called jumbo jets.

JETS

All jets have a main part called the body. They have long wings, too. The front of the jet is called the nose. Most **commercial** (*kuh-MER-shul*) jets have wide bodies. Other jets have **narrow** bodies.

A jet called the Boeing (*BOH-wing*) 747 is a famous jumbo jet

People can fly jets high in the air. At first, jets could fly 10,000 feet (3,048 m) above the ground. But now jets can fly about 50,000 feet (15,240 m) above the ground. The pilot controls the jet. He or she sits in the **cockpit**.

Fuselage (*FEW-suh-lahj*) is another name for the body of a jet

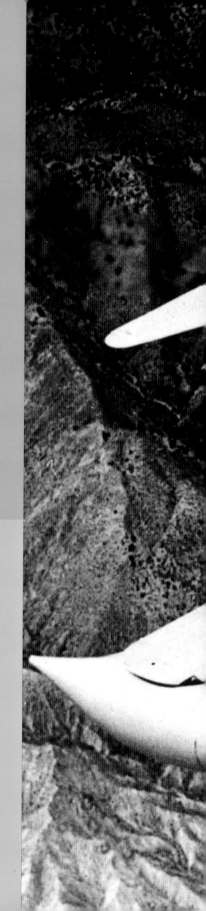

The first jet engines were made in the 1930s. Some of the first jets were built in Great Britain. They were used by the military as fighter planes. These jets had guns on them.

Fighter jets have nicknames, such as this "Shooting Star"

When a jumbo jet is ready to land, it puts down its wheels

Today, there are many kinds of jets. Most commercial jets are used to carry people. Jumbo jets and jetliners are usually commercial jets.

JETS

Some people who take short trips ride in small jetliners. Militaries use jets, too. Fighter jets are smaller jets. Fighter jets have room for only one or two people.

18

Fighter jets (above) are even smaller than jetliners (opposite)

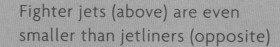

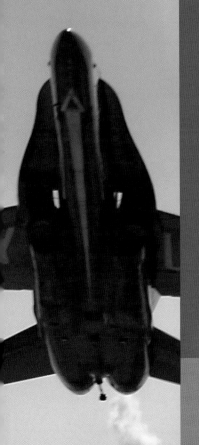

When jets fly, they can go anywhere in the world. Passenger jets fly above the clouds. Fighter jets can go in loops and shoot down enemy airplanes.

Fighter jets sometimes fly together in a group called a formation

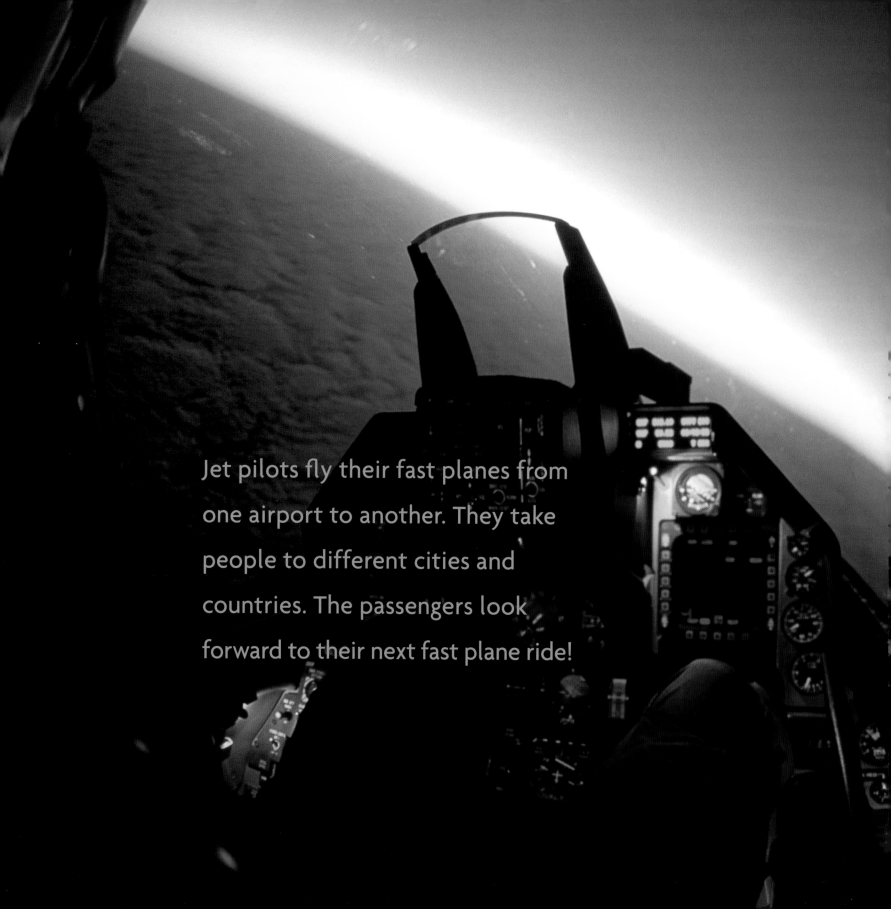

Jet pilots fly their fast planes from one airport to another. They take people to different cities and countries. The passengers look forward to their next fast plane ride!

Fast Facts

Pilots in the United States Air Force fly lots of fighter jets called F-22 Raptors.

Wide jets such as jumbo jets can carry between 200 and 600 passengers.

An English man named Frank Whittle was one of the first jet engine **inventors**.

The X-15 was one of the fastest jets ever. It went more than 4,000 miles (6,437 km) per hour!

Glossary

cockpit—the place where the pilot sits in an airplane

commercial—something that is used to make money

engines—machines inside vehicles that make them move

inventors—people who come up with new ideas and make new things

narrow—skinny; not wide

passengers—people who ride on a jet or other vehicle

Read More about It

Braulick, Carrie. *Jets*. Mankato, Minn.: Capstone Press, 2007

Schaefer, A. R. *Jet Fighter Planes*. Mankato, Minn.: Capstone Press, 2005.

Web Site

Boeing Kids Page
http://www.boeing.com/companyoffices/aboutus/kids/coloring.html
This site has pictures of jets that can be colored.

Index